DUT
CHRISTIAN FELLOWSHIP

A Manual for Church Members

John Owen

*Modernized and with
Questions Added for Discussion*

THE BANNER OF TRUTH TRUST

DUTIES OF
CHRISTIAN FELLOWSHIP

ESHCOL:
A CLUSTER OF THE GRAPES OF CANAAN

*Brought to the Borders for the Encouragement
of the Saints Travelling to the Land,
with Their Faces Toward Zion*

Or

*Rules for Directing Believers How to Walk
in Fellowship According to
the Order of the Gospel*

THE BANNER OF TRUTH TRUST

3 Murrayfield Road, Edinburgh EH12 6EL, UK
PO Box 621, Carlisle, PA 17013, USA

*

ISBN:
Print: 978 1 84871 772 5
Epub: 978 1 84871 773 2
Kindle: 978 1 84871 775 6

*

Typeset in 11/14 pt Adobe Garamond Pro at
The Banner of Truth Trust
Printed in the USA by
VersaPress, Inc.,
East Peoria, IL

Contents

This little book was first published in 1647 soon after Owen had formed a church on Independent principles at Coggleshall, in Essex…. It was prepared by [the] author after he had adopted Congregational views but is of such a nature as to be applicable and useful under any form of [church government]. Each rule is established by a body of evidence from Scripture and is followed by a general explanation.

Several editions of this work have been published. And we are not surprised at its favourable reception by believers, for it is as remarkable as any work by the author for deep piety, sound judgement, lucid arrangement, and a comprehensive knowledge of Scripture. It forms a manual of church-fellowship which is to this day unsurpassed. One feature of it can hardly escape the reader's attention—John Owen is here, for once, a master in the art of concise writing.

WILLIAM H. GOOLD
1850

Suggestions for the Use of this Book

JOHN OWEN wrote this manual originally, it is presumed, for individual use. The very personal nature of the godly living for which he is arguing requires self-examination, meditation and prayer, and the study of the book is therefore, perhaps, best carried out privately. Individuals might wish to concentrate on one rule, with its Scripture verses and explanation, as the focus of their thoughts and prayers during a particular day. There is, indeed, sufficient content in each of its twenty-two rules for it to serve as the basis of meditation and further elaboration for a week. Here then is a manual that a believer might use for a brief three-week study or for longer consideration over a five-month period.

But as a manual for church fellowship, the booklet is ideal for the combined attention of the church. With a copy of the text available for all members, each rule might be taken up as a topic for a week-day Bible study or for an adult Sunday School class. The pastor of the church might perhaps feel uncomfortable in leading the studies for the first section of rules which treat the relationship of members and pastor, but this might be taken up by an elder, retired minister, etc., leaving the second fifteen-rule section to the pastor. Such studies might very usefully be concluded with question and answer, and/or discussion periods.

Many churches now arrange house-groups of smaller numbers for Bible study and discussion. With copies available for each member so that they might prepare thoughtfully for the meeting, one or two rules could be profitably considered during each session. If the group meets weekly this might result in a ten-week study; monthly, it might occupy discussions for a year.

Questions have been added to the text to facilitate discussion. They do not in any way provide a complete review of the content of each section but focus on some specific points. Some of the more personal questions might best be left for individual consideration rather than for group discussion.

The sensitivity and love towards one another which is essential for church fellowship, and for which John Owen argued so urgently, would, of course, be a necessary requirement for all participating in such discussions whether in a church meeting or in smaller groups.

Foreword

CERTAIN principles with respect to the management of churches are agreed upon by all who long for the increase of the power of godliness, though they might belong to different denominations and persuasions. Four of the most important of those principles, upon which the rules in this book are based, are:

1. The gathering together of individual assemblies or congregations of believers, under the leadership of their officers, so that they might participate in the ordinances of Jesus Christ, is a divine institution.

2. Every faithful believer is bound to join himself to some such single congregation that displays the notes and marks of a true church.

3. Each believer's voluntary consent and submission to the ordinances of Christ in that church is required before he may join with it and have fellowship in it.

4. It is convenient for all believers living in one place to join themselves into one congregation, unless through sheer numbers more congregations are required. Otherwise there is the danger of strife, envy, and breach of love.

The following pages, building on the above principles, seek to draw believers from the entanglements of arguments about church matters and to engage them in the serious and humble performance of those duties which are, by the express command of Christ, required of us all.

> For this is the will of God, that by doing good you should put to silence the ignorance of foolish people (1 Pet. 2:15).

Questions for consideration/discussion

1. John Owen's title for this manual was *Eshcol* (see above p. 3). Why do you think he chose that title? (Num. 13:23-24)

2. He wrote the manual for church members of the seventeenth century (it was published in 1647). Why should his rules still apply to believers of the twenty-first century?

3. Do you think that the four principles mentioned are still generally agreed upon?

SECTION ONE

Rules for walking in fellowship with respect
to the pastor of the congregation, with
explanations of the rules, and motives for
keeping them (Rules 1-7)

Rule 1

Believers are to attend regularly, and to submit to, the preaching of the word and administering of the ordinances committed to the pastor by virtue of his ministerial office. They are to do this with a willing obedience in the Lord.

- 1 Cor. 4:1. This is how one should regard us, as servants of Christ and stewards of the mysteries of God.

- 2 Cor. 5:18, 20. God… gave us the ministry of reconciliation…. Therefore, we are ambassadors for Christ, God making his appeal through us.

- 2 Cor. 4:7. But we have this treasure in jars of clay, to show that the surpassing power belongs to God and not to us; see also 2 Cor. 6:1.

- Gal. 4:14. [You] received me as an angel of God, as Christ Jesus.

- 2 Thess. 3:14. If anyone does not obey what we say in this letter, take note of that person, and have nothing to do with him.

- Heb. 13:7, 17. Remember your leaders, those who spoke to you the word of God.... Obey your leaders and submit to them, for they are keeping watch over your souls, as those who will have to give an account. Let them do this with joy and not with groaning, for that would be of no advantage to you.

Explanation 1

There is a two-fold power provided for the preaching of the word: *ability* and *authority*.

The first, the *ability* to preach, with its required qualifications (mentioned in 1 Tim. 3:2-7; Titus 1:6-9) needs to be present in those called to the office of minister; and may be also, in varying degrees, in those not set apart to the office but warranted by it to preach the gospel when called upon to do so in God's providence, Rom. 10:14-15. In that the work of preaching for the conversion of souls is a moral duty contained under the general precept of doing good to all, it is not confined only to those who are appointed to it by office.

The second, the *authority* possessed by those who are formally set apart, arises from:

1. Christ's institution of the office, Eph. 4:11.

2. God's providential appointing of the persons, Matt. 9:38.

3. The church's call, election, appointment, acceptance and submission, Gal. 4:14; Acts 14:23; 1 Thess. 5:12-13;

Acts 6:3; 2 Cor. 8:5. These do not give pastors the right to rule over the faith of believers, 2 Cor. 1:24, nor make them lords over God's heritage, 1 Pet. 5:3, but entrust to them the power of a steward in God's house, 1 Cor. 4:1-2, that is, the particular flock over which they have been made overseers, Acts 20:28.

From such men the word is to be received:

1. As the truth of God.

2. As the truth proclaimed with ministerial authority to themselves in particular, according to Christ's institution.

The failure to consider these principles is the cause of all the negligence, carelessness, laziness, and indiscipline while hearing the word, which has taken hold of so many these days. Only a respect for the truth and authority of God in the preaching of his word will bring men to hear it soberly and profitably. It is also the case that men grow tired of hearing the word only after they have grown tired of putting it into practice.

Some motives for obeying this rule arise from an acknowledgement of:

1. The One in whose name pastors speak and preach, 2 Cor. 5:20.

2. The work which they do, 1 Cor. 3:9; 2 Cor. 6:1; 1 Tim. 4:16.

3. The account that they will have to give, Heb. 13:17.

4. The regard that God has for them as they work for him, Matt. 10:40; Luke 10:16.

5. The account that the hearers must give of the word which was preached to them, 2 Chron. 36:15-16; Prov. 1:22-29; Luke 10:16; Mark 4:24; Heb. 2:1-3, 4:2.

Questions for consideration/discussion

1. In our day and age, there is an undercurrent of rebellion against all forms of authority. How does this manifest itself in the attitudes of (i) unbelievers, (ii) believers, to God's servant—the pastor?

2. Do we distinguish between the pastor with respect to his heavenly office and divine calling, and the pastor as a sinful man? How do we maintain the balance between these two aspects of a pastor's life, in our relationship with him?

3. In the light of these rules, how should a believer listen to a sermon from his pastor?

4. Many church-life issues are involved in this rule: regularity of attendance at services; subsequent meditation upon the content of a sermon, for example. List and discuss other such issues that you may think of.

Rule 2

The pastor's way of life is to be observed and carefully followed, to the extent that he walks in the ways of Jesus Christ.

- 1 Cor. 4:16. I urge you, then, be imitators of me.

- 1 Cor. 11:1. Be imitators of me, as I am of Christ.

- Heb. 13:7. Remember your leaders, those who spoke to you the word of God. Consider the outcome of their way of life, and imitate their faith.

- 2 Thess. 3:7. For you yourselves know how you ought to imitate us, because we were not idle when we were with you.

- Phil. 3:17. Brothers, join in imitating me, and keep your eyes on those who walk according to the example you have in us.

- 1 Tim. 4:12. Set the believers an example in speech, in conduct, in love, in faith, in purity.

- 1 Pet. 5:3. Being examples to the flock.

Explanation 2

It is clear that an exemplary life was always required in those who administered holy things, both under the Old and the New Testaments. The glorious robes of the Old Testament priests, the uprightness and integrity of their lives without imperfections or blemishes, the Urim and the Thummim, the many other ornaments, all these were in the first place types of Jesus Christ, yet they also clearly displayed the purity and holiness required in those who ministered, Zech. 3:4. In the New Testament, it is clearly commanded that the light of their good works should shine, Matt. 5:16. This is so, not only to ensure that no offence to God's ways and worship is given by those who minister them (as occurred in both Testaments, 1 Sam. 2:17; Phil. 3:18-19), but also that unbelievers might be convinced (1 Tim. 3:7) and the churches given an example of the practical living out of God's mind and will.

A pastor's life should be vocal: sermons must be lived out as well as preached. Though Noah's men built the ark, yet they themselves were drowned. God will not accept our tongues when the devil has our hearts. Jesus did both 'do and teach', Acts 1:1. If a man teaches uprightly but walks crookedly, more will fall down in the night of his life than he built in the day of his doctrine.

The fulfilling of an exemplary life in a minister requires that the life of Christ should be in him, Gal. 2:20, so that when he has taught others he himself should not be disqualified, 1 Cor. 9:27. It is this life which provides for him a spiritual understanding and gives him a light into God's counsels, which he is then to communicate to others, 1 John 5:20; 1 Cor. 2:12-13; 2 Cor. 4:6-7. It is a distinctive life, Matt. 5:46; Luke 6:32; one for which many personal qualifications and duties are required, 1 Tim. 3:1-7; Titus

1:6-9. He is to aim at being an example so as to bring glory to God, 1 Tim. 4:12.

Therefore the pastor's way of life and the outcome of his faith are to be observed, Heb. 13:7. His weaknesses, whilst real and evident as he is exposed to many temptations and opposed by many adversaries, are to be covered with love, Gal. 4:13-14. And this will be done if the flock recognizes conscientiously that their teacher's life is a means of grace from God provided as a relief for them when under temptation, and an encouragement to holiness, zeal, meekness and self-denial.

Questions for consideration/discussion

1. Do you take your pastor as a role model? What would you learn, as a rebuke to your own way of life, following a fair and honest review of your pastor's life?

2. In what ways would your church be different if all members were to imitate the pastor in his areas of strength?

3. '*His weaknesses ... are to be covered with love.*' Do you do this? How should a church, or indeed an individual church member, best deal with a perceived weakness in the pastor?

4. Put yourself in your pastor's shoes. What pressures and stresses would you experience, knowing that the eye of the church was upon you?

Rule 3

Prayer and supplications are to be made continually on the pastor's behalf that he might receive help and success in the work that has been given to him.

- Eph. 6:18-20. Praying at all times in the Spirit, with all prayer and supplication. To that end, keep alert with all perseverance, making supplication for all the saints, and also for me, that words may be given to me in opening my mouth boldly to proclaim the mystery of the gospel, for which I am an ambassador.

- 2 Thess. 3:1-2. Finally, brothers, pray for us, that the word of the Lord may speed ahead and be honoured … and that we may be delivered from wicked and evil men; 1 Thess. 5:25.

- Col. 4:3. Pray also for us, that God may open to us a door for the word, to declare the mystery of Christ; Heb. 13:18.

- Acts 12:5. Earnest prayer for him was made to God by the church; Heb. 13:7.

Explanation 3

The greatness of the work (for who is sufficient for it? 2 Cor. 2:16); the strength of the opposition to it, 1 Cor. 16:9; Rev. 12:12; 2 Tim. 4:3-5; its involvement in the fate of men's souls, Acts 20:26-28; Heb. 13:17; 1 Tim. 4:16; the conviction which is to be brought upon the world by it, Ezek. 2:5; 1 Cor. 1:23-24; 2 Cor. 3:15-16; its aim and tendency to the glory of God in Christ—these all call out for the most effectual daily involvement of the saints in their supplications for its support. The rule requires that prayer be made for assistance, encouragement, abilities, success, deliverance and protection. As the temptations experienced by pastors increase, so must the prayers on their behalf. There are many curses made against them, Jer. 15:10; the hope is that God hears the prayers made for them. When many are not ashamed to revile them in public, some ought to be ashamed for not remembering them in private.

Motives for obeying this rule:

1. The preached word will certainly be effectual when the ability to preach it is supplied as a result of prayer, Acts 10:1-6.

2. The failure of a minister is a punishment of the people, Amos 8:11-12; Isa. 30:20.

3. The pastor prays for the church continually, Isa. 62:6-7; Rom. 1:9-10.

4. The great need of the pastor for prayer is not for his own good but for the saints' good. Help the one who carries the burden, Eph. 6:18-20; Phil. 2:17; Col. 1:24.

> *Questions for consideration/discussion*
>
> 1. One of the main burdens of any church prayer-meeting should be for God's blessing on the pastor of the church and on all the ministers of the land. Is this the case generally?
>
> 2. The same is true for the believer's daily prayers. Again, is this the case?
>
> 3. Is it realised that any perceived weakness in the pastor's ministry may be due to the prayerlessness of the church?

Rule 4

Believers are to hold the pastor in the greatest respect and to submit to him, for the work's sake.

- 1 Cor. 4:1. This is how one should regard us, as servants of Christ and stewards of the mysteries of God.

- 1 Thess. 5:12-13. We ask you, brothers, to respect those who labour among you and are over you in the Lord and admonish you, and to esteem them very highly in love because of their work.

- 1 Tim. 5:17. Let the elders who rule well be considered worthy of double honour, especially those who labour in preaching and teaching.

- 1 Pet. 5:5. Be subject to the elders.

- Heb. 13:17. Obey your leaders and submit to them.

Explanation 4

The esteem that is required by this rule is that of a civil, respectful esteem, but the motive for it is sacred. That a pastor is honoured reveals the grace of a church, and to be respectful of him is a gospel duty, acceptable to God in Christ, 1 Tim. 5:17. Honour and reverence is due wherever there is eminence and distinction. This is given to pastors by their office and proved by their titles. They are called 'angels', Rev. 1:20; Heb. 12:22; 'bishops', or 'overseers', Ezek. 3:17; Acts 20:28; Titus 1:7; 'ambassadors', 2 Cor. 5:20; 'stewards', 1 Cor. 4:1; 'men of God', 1 Sam. 2:27; 1 Tim. 6:11; 'leaders', Heb. 13:7, 17; 'lights', Matt. 5:14; 'salt', Matt. 5:13; 'fathers', 1 Cor. 4:15; and many other similar titles. If, according to these names, they honour God as they ought, God will also honour them as he has promised, and God's people, in all conscience, are to esteem them highly for their work's sake. But if any of them are fallen angels, falling stars, negligent bishops, treacherous ambassadors, lordly revelling stewards, tyrannical or foolish leaders, blind guides or unsavoury salt, the Lord and his people will abhor them.

Questions for consideration/discussion

1. How does this scriptural respect for the pastor manifest itself in practice?

2. As in Question 2 for Rule 1, how do we hold the balance between respect for the pastor for his work and office's sake, and an objective evaluation of his faithfulness and effectiveness in the work?

3. Discuss all that is involved in the scriptural submission of a church member to his or her pastor, as to its extent and also its limits.

Rule 5

The church is required to support the pastor and his family by supplying all their earthly needs, to the degree that is appropriate to the state and condition of the church.

- 1 Tim. 5:17-18. Let the elders who rule well be considered worthy of double honour, especially those who labour in preaching and teaching. For the Scripture says, 'You shall not muzzle an ox when it treads out the grain', and 'The labourer deserves his wages'.

- Gal. 6:6-7. One who is taught the word must share all good things with the one who teaches. Do not be deceived: God is not mocked, for whatever one sows, that will he also reap.

- 1 Cor. 9:7, 9-11, 13-14. Who serves as a soldier at his own expense? Who plants a vineyard without eating any of its fruit? Or who tends a flock without getting some of the milk?... For it is written in the law of Moses, 'You shall not muzzle an ox when it treads out the grain.' Is it for oxen that God is concerned? Does he not speak entirely for our sake? It was written for our sake, because the ploughman should plough in hope and the thresher thresh in hope of sharing in the crop. If we have sown spiritual things among you, is it too much if we reap material things from you?... Do you not know that those who are employed in the temple service get their food from the temple, and those who serve at the altar share in the sacrificial offerings? In the same way, the Lord commanded that those who proclaim the gospel should get their living by the gospel.

- Matt. 10:9-10. Acquire no gold nor silver nor copper for your belts, no bag for your journey, nor two tunics nor sandals nor a staff, for the labourer deserves his food.

Add to these, and similar verses, the analogy of the taxes paid in the Jewish church.

Explanation 5

There is a promise to the church under the gospel, that 'kings shall be your foster fathers, and their queens your nursing mothers', Isa. 49:23. The responsibility for providing food and protection for those committed to serve the churches of the land lies firstly upon those in authority. The churches have enjoyed the fruit of this promise in many ages; laws have been enacted by supreme and kingly powers, giving portions and granting privileges to churches and their pastors. It is so in many places today. In such cases, where equitable and righteous laws have allowed material support to the pastors of churches, who, in their turn, provide spiritual benefits by their labours in the gospel, this is to be accepted and embraced thankfully, as an issue of God's providence for his own. The Saviour allowed his disciples to receive their support from those to whom they preached, Luke 10:8.

But this is not always the case; such arrangements may fail. Therefore, the continual care and burden, or rather the labour of love, for providing for pastors lies, as a rule, upon the churches themselves. They are to do this in a way which is appropriate to their situations and to the financial position in which God has placed them. Each church in general, and each member in particular, is obliged to do this.

Motives for obeying this rule:

1. It is God's *command*, as shown in the texts above.

2. The *necessity* of it. How shall the pastor 'serve as a soldier' if he is worrying about the necessities of life? They are to give themselves wholly to this spiritual work, 1 Tim. 4:15; any other necessary material and temporal works should be done for them.

3. The *fairness* of it. Our Saviour and the apostles argued for it on the basis of equity and justice, and of various human laws and rules of righteousness, Matt. 10:9-10; 1 Cor. 9:10.

To fail to provide a proportionate wage for the labourer is a crying sin, James 5:4-5. It is the wretched efforts of corrupt men to rob, or reduce the value, of that which pastors, by God's providence, have every right to receive.

Questions for consideration/discussion

1. Do you agree with John Owen that it is, ideally, the duty of the State to support the church's ministry? Would this be the case also for the ministries of other religions as well as Christianity?

2. What does John Owen mean by the italicised words in the phrase, 'supplying all their earthly needs, *to the degree that is appropriate to the state and condition of the church*'? How could a church evaluate this appropriate degree?

Rule 6

The church is to remain loyal to the pastor and to stay at his side in all the trials and persecutions that may arise because of the word.

- 2 Tim. 4:16. At my first defence no one came to stand by me, but all deserted me. May it not be charged against them!

- 1 Tim. 2:16-18. May the Lord grant mercy to the

household of Onesiphorus, for he often refreshed me and was not ashamed of my chains, but when he arrived in Rome he searched for me earnestly and found me—may the Lord grant him to find mercy from the Lord on that Day!—and you well know all the service he rendered at Ephesus.

Explanation 6

A common cause should be carried out by a common effort. What concerns everybody should be supported by everybody. When persecution arises for the word's sake it generally begins with the leaders, 1 Pet. 4:17-18. The usual way to scatter the sheep is by smiting the shepherd, Zech. 13:7-8. It is because of the church that he is reviled and persecuted, 2 Tim. 2:10; Col. 1:24, and therefore it is the duty of the church to share his burden and help him carry it.

When churches are scattered, the whole blame does not lie on the ministers; the people did not stand by them when the trial came. May it not be charged against them! When a captain, advancing against danger, looks back expecting to see his soldiers with him but finds that they have run away, he is greatly betrayed and forced into an impossible position by his enemies.

In England, generally, no sooner had persecution laid hold of a minister, than the people willingly received another man, perhaps a wolf, instead of their shepherd. Should a wife leave her husband because he is in some trouble for her sake? When the duty of a husband or wife in such a position is clear, is it less of a crime for a backslider in spiritual things? When a pastor is still alive, suffering for the truth, a church cannot desert him, nor stop fulfilling all their required duties towards him, without being guilty of a wicked contempt of the ordinances of Jesus Christ. This is a burden that is often laid on the shoulders of ministers, that for no reason of their own they are forced to leave their charge, whilst those who lay the burden upon them will often freely leave them and their ministry for no reason at all.

Questions for consideration/discussion

1. What are the distinctive burdens, trials and persecutions that a pastor today may suffer '*because of the word*'?

2. What are the practical steps that a church should take in order (a) to be aware of and sensitive to the existence of these burdens, and (b) to relieve the pastor who is feeling the weight of them?

Rule 7

Believers, along with their families, must gather together as a congregation before the pastor, at the times appointed by him.

- Acts 14:27. And when they arrived and gathered the church together.

Questions for consideration/discussion

1. Clearly John Owen believed that pastors had the authority to decide when and how often the congregation should be gathered together. Today, in many cases, it is the congregation rather than the church officers that decide this. Is there any scriptural principle involved here?

---

* * *

These are some of the areas where the church has a duty towards him, or them, who are set over it in the Lord, encouraging them in their work in every way possible. Saying to them, also, 'See that you fulfil the ministry that you have received in the Lord', Col. 4:17.

Whatever might be appropriate also to church officers other than the pastor may be understood from these seven rules.

SECTION TWO

Rules for walking in fellowship with respect
to other believers, with explanations of the
rules, and motives for keeping them
(Rules 1-15)

Rule 1

Believers have a duty of affectionate, sincere, genuine love in all things towards one another; a love compared to that of Christ for the church.

- John 15:12. This is my commandment, that you love one another as I have loved you.

- John 13:34-35. A new commandment I give to you, that you love one another: just as I have loved you, you also are to love one another. By this all people will know that you are my disciples, if you have love for one another.

- Rom. 13:8. Owe no one anything, except to love each other, for the one who loves another has fulfilled the law.

- Eph. 5:2. Walk in love, as Christ loved us.

- 1 Thess. 3:12. May the Lord make you increase and abound in love for one another.

- 1 Thess. 4:9. You yourselves have been taught by God to love one another.

- 1 Pet. 1:22. Having purified your souls by your obedience to the truth for a sincere brotherly love, love one another earnestly from a pure heart.

- 1 John 4:21. This commandment we have from him: whoever loves God must also love his brother.

- Rom. 12:10. Love one another with brotherly affection.

Explanation 1

Love is the fountain of all duties towards God and man, Matt. 22:37-39, the basis of all rules that concern the saints, the bond of communion, the 'fulfilling of the law', Rom. 13:8-10, the advancement of the honour of the Lord Jesus, and the glory of the gospel. The early Christians had a proverbial saying, received, according to tradition, from Christ: 'Never rejoice except when, with love, you see your brother.' And unbelievers would commonly say of them, 'See how they love one another!' because of their willingness to obey that royal rule of laying down their lives for their brothers. It is the fountain, rule, scope, aim, and fruit of gospel communion.

The teaching of the Lord Jesus emphasises no other virtue as highly as that of mutual, intense, affectionate love amongst his followers. To this end he gives innumerable precepts, exhortations, motivations and, above all, his own heavenly example. To discuss love in its causes, nature, subject, fruit, effects, tendency, eminence and exaltation, or merely to quote the Scriptures where these things are mentioned, would not fit in with our present purpose. But it may be safely stated that if there was no other purpose for reforming and improving our mutual fellowship than this purpose—the recovery of the power and practice of the grace of mutual love—that should be encouragement enough to undertake it whatever the opposition. At present it is a grace that, shamefully, has been lost amongst those who call themselves Christians, to the dishonour of Christ and his gospel.

This love is a spiritual grace, wrought by the Holy Spirit in the hearts of believers, Gal. 5:22; 1 Pet. 1:22; by which their souls are drawn out to seek the good of God's children, 1 Thess. 2:8; Philem. 5; Eph. 1:15; Heb. 13:1. It unites our hearts to those we thus love and is accompanied by a joy, a delight and a satisfaction at seeing them blessed.

Motives for obeying this rule:

1. The *command of God*, and the nature of the whole law—for 'love is the fulfilling of the law'. Lev. 19:34; Matt. 19:19; Rom. 13:8-10.

2. The eternal, distinguishing *faithful love of God* towards believers and his purpose in it, Ezek. 16:8; Deut. 7:8; 33:3; Zeph. 3:17; Rom. 5:8; Eph. 1:4.

3. The intense, *inexpressible love of Jesus Christ*, seen in his humiliation and in his laying down of his life for us, presented to us as an example, Song of Sol. 3:10; John 15:13; Eph. 5:2.

4. The notable *renewal of the old command to love*, with such reinforcement that it is called 'a new commandment', and is distinctively the law of Christ, John 13:34; 15:12; 1 Thess. 4:9; 2 John 5.

5. The state and condition of those between whom this duty is to be naturally fulfilled, namely, (a) children of one Father, Mal. 2:10; (b) members of one body, 1 Cor. 12:12-13; (c) partakers of the same hope, Eph. 4:4; (d) objects of the same hate of the world, 1 John 3:13.

6. The pre-eminence of this grace: (a) in itself, and in its divine nature, Col. 2:2; 1 John 4:7; 1 Cor. 13; (b) in its usefulness, Prov. 10:12; 15:17; Gal. 5:13; Heb. 13:1; (c) in its acceptance with believers, Eph. 1:15-16; Psa. 5:11; 1 Cor. 13.

7. The impossibility of performing any other duty without it, 1 Cor. 13:1-3; Gal. 5:6; 1 Thess. 1:3; 1 John 4:20.

8. The great sin of lack of love, with all its consequences, Matt. 24:12; 1 John 3:14-15, and similar verses.

It is love, the bond of communion, which manifests itself and is active in all the rules that follow.

Questions for consideration/discussion

1. John Owen believed that in his day mutual love was a grace *'that, shamefully, has been lost amongst those who call themselves Christians, to the dishonour of Christ and his gospel.'* Is this true today, or not?

2. The comment is sometimes heard, 'We do not have to like all other believers, but to love them.' Is this a valid distinction?

3. When this necessary grace of love is weak among us, how do we restore it?

4. In the light of John 13:35, discuss the connection between the expression of this love and evangelism. Have you had experiences of the effectiveness of this form of Christian witness?

Rule 2

Believers must maintain continual prayer for the prospering of the church under God's protection.

- Psa. 122:6. Pray for the peace of Jerusalem! May they be secure who love you!

- Phil. 1:4-5. Always in every prayer of mine for you all making my prayer with joy, because of your partnership in the gospel from the first day until now.

- Rom. 1:9-10. Without ceasing I mention you always in my prayers.

- Acts 12:5. Peter was kept in prison, but earnest prayer for him was made to God by the church.

- Isa. 62:6-7. You who put the LORD in remembrance, take no rest, and give him no rest until he establishes Jerusalem and makes it a praise in the earth.

- Eph. 6:18. Praying at all times in the Spirit, with all prayer and supplication. To that end keep alert with all perseverance, making supplication for all the saints.

- Col. 4:12. Epaphras, who is one of you, a servant of Christ Jesus, greets you, always struggling on your behalf in his prayers, that you may stand mature and fully assured in all the will of God.

Explanation 2

Just as prayer is the great means of prevailing with the Almighty, Isa. 45:11, so it is the sure refuge of the saints at all times, both for their own behalf, Psa. 61:2, and also for others, Acts 12:5. It is a benefit which the poorest believer may bestow, and the greatest potentate has no power to refuse. This is the well-trodden path of the soul's communion with God and for which the saints have many gracious promises of help, Zech. 12:10; Rom. 8:26; innumerable precepts to perform, Matt. 7:7; 1 Thess. 5:17; 1 Tim. 2:8; many encouragements, James 1:5; Luke 11:9; and precious promises of acceptance, Matt. 21:22; John 16:24; Psa. 50:15. By these and many other ways, the Lord has abundantly witnessed to his delight in this sacrifice of his people.

Now, as believers are called upon to pray for all men, of every kind, 1 Tim. 2:1-2, (except for those who have committed the sin leading to death, 1 John 5:16) even for their persecutors, Matt. 5:44, and those who enslave them, Jer. 29:7, so they must especially pray for all saints, Phil. 1:4, and particularly for those with whom they are in fellowship, Col. 4:12. The Lord has promised that 'over the whole site of Mount Zion and over her assemblies' there shall be 'a cloud by day, and smoke and the shining of a flaming fire by night', Isa. 4:5, and it is the duty of all to pray that this should be the case. Someone who does not continue in prayer for the protection of the church is not worthy of the church's privileges. Prayer, therefore, for the good, prosperity, flourishing, peace, increase, edification and protection of the church is a duty required from all its members.

Motives for obeying this rule:

1. Respect for the ordinances of God.

2. Concern for God's glory.

3. The honour of Jesus Christ.

4. Our own benefit and spiritual interest.

5. The directness of the commands.

Questions for consideration/discussion

1. Again (see Section 1, Rule 3, Question 1), here is a burden that should be expressed in every church prayer-meeting, and daily in every believer's prayers. Is this the case?

---

2. How should we interpret, and act on, the *'take no rest and give him no rest'* of Isaiah 62?

3. What exactly should we be praying for, in seeking the prosperity of the church?

Rule 3

Believers must strive and fight with determination, in every legitimate way, by their actions and sufferings, for the purity of the ordinances, for the honour, liberty and privileges of the congregation, and in order to help others in the face of all opponents and adversaries.

- Jude 3. Appealing to you to contend for the faith that was once for all delivered to the saints.

- Heb. 12:3-4. Consider him who endured from sinners such hostility against himself, so that you may not grow weary or faint-hearted. In your struggle against sin you have not yet resisted to the point of shedding your blood.

- 1 John 3:16. By this we know love, that he laid down his life for us, and we ought to lay down our lives for the brothers.

- Gal. 5:1, 13. For freedom Christ has set us free; stand firm therefore, and do not submit again to a yoke of slavery... For you were called to freedom, brothers.

- 1 Cor. 7:23. You were bought with a price; do not become slaves of men.

- Song of Sol. 6:4. You are beautiful... my love... awesome as an army with banners.

- 1 Pet. 3:15. Always being prepared to make a defence to anyone who asks you for a reason for the hope that is in you; yet do it with gentleness and respect.

Explanation 3

The previous rule had to do with our dealings with God on behalf of the church; this rule involves our dealings with men. Fulfilling this rule correctly requires many things, such as:

1. Diligent study in the word, with fervent prayer, to learn the mind and will of God as to how we are to worship and how we are to live, so that we might be able to explain this to humble inquirers and to stop the mouths of stubborn opponents. We will value the ordinances that we enjoy according to the degree of knowledge of them that we possess. A man will not contend unless he knows what he is fighting for.

2. The understanding that all the criticisms of, and the injuries made to the church, are in fact criticisms of, and injuries made to Christ and, also, to ourselves—

Christ wounded through the sides of his servants and his ways. And if we are his, though the blow might not fall directly upon us, yet we feel the pain of it; all such reproaches and rebukes fall on us.

3. A just vindication of the church against all false criticisms and allegations. Who could bear hearing his earthly parents being falsely accused? In the same way, we should oppose all the false criticisms made against the church—our heavenly mother who bears us to Christ.

4. A common repudiation, with all gospel opposition, of any person or thing which strives, against the word, and by whatever name, for power over the church; seeking to curtail any of its freedoms and privileges which Christ has won for it. To those who would bring us captive we should not submit for a moment.

Questions for consideration/discussion

1. What are the present-day examples of the *'opponents and adversaries'*, both of believers individually and of the church generally?

2. What dangers must we guard against when fighting the fight of faith?

3. What light does the teaching of, (a) 2 Cor. 10:4-6, and (b) Rom. 12:18, shed on this duty of spiritual warfare?

4. In Explanation 1, John Owen suggests that the maintenance of true worship is something to be fought for. What are the essential principles of worship for which we should contend?

Rule 4

Believers must maintain an unremitting care and effort to preserve unity, both in general and in particular.

- Phil. 2:1-3. So if there is any encouragement in Christ, any comfort from love, any participation in the Spirit, any affection and sympathy, complete my joy by being of the same mind, having the same love, being in full accord and of one mind. Do nothing from rivalry or conceit, but in humility count others more significant than yourselves.

- Eph. 4:3-6. Eager to maintain the unity of the Spirit in the bond of peace. There is one body and one Spirit— just as you were called to the one hope that belongs to your call—one Lord, one faith, one baptism, one God and Father of all, who is over all and through all and in all.

- 1 Cor. 1:10. I appeal to you, brothers, by the name of our Lord Jesus Christ, that all of you agree, and that there be no divisions among you, but that you be united in the same mind and the same judgement.

- 2 Cor. 13:11. Aim for restoration, comfort one another, agree with one another, live in peace; and the God of love and peace will be with you.

- Rom. 14:19. So then let us pursue what makes for peace and for mutual upbuilding.

- Rom. 15:5-6. May the God of endurance and encouragement grant you to live in such harmony with one another, in accord with Christ Jesus, that together you may with one voice glorify the God and Father of our Lord Jesus Christ.

- 1 Cor. 6:5-7. Can it be that there is no one among you wise enough to settle a dispute between the brothers, but brother goes to law against brother, and that before unbelievers? To have lawsuits at all with one another is already a defeat for you.

- Acts 4:32. Now the full number of those who believed were of one heart and soul.

Explanation 4

Unity is the main aim, and the most appropriate fruit, of love. There is no other Christian duty urged with more earnestness and vehemence than that of unity. Unity is threefold:

Firstly, *spiritual unity*, brought about by the participation of the same Spirit of grace, by communion with Christ—the one head over all. We have this unity with all the saints in the world, whatever their condition; yes, even with those who have departed and now sit down in the kingdom of heaven with Abraham, Isaac and Jacob.

Secondly, *ecclesiastical or church unity*, as we participate in the ordinances appointed in the gospel. This is a fruit and branch of spiritual unity. It opposes schism, divisions, splits, suspicious speculations, maverick customs, unnecessary differences in judgment on spiritual things concerning the kingdom of Christ, and whatever else which draws us away from close affection, unity of mind, consent in judgment to agreed confessions, conformity of practice to scriptural rule. It is what is so earnestly urged upon the churches: commanded and desired as that which is to the glory of Christ, the honour of the gospel, and the joy and crown of the saints.

Thirdly, *civil unity*, or an agreement in the things of this life: not fighting for them or about them, but with every man seeking the welfare of the other. Striving is not appropriate for brethren. Why should they who shall together judge the world strive against one another?

Motives for obeying this rule:

1. The remarkable earnestness of Christ and the apostles in their prayers and directions with respect to this duty.

2. The certain dishonour of the Lord Jesus, the scandal to the gospel, the ruin of churches, and the shame and sorrow to the saints, that will arise when this duty is neglected, Gal. 5:15.

3. The gracious results and the sweet heavenly comforts that flow from preserving unity.

4. The many fearful distresses which always result from the sin of rending the body of Christ.

5. The sad contempt and profaning of the ordinances which often occurs when there is lack of unity

To fulfil this duty we must:

1. Labour, by prayer and faith, to have our hearts and spirits thoroughly seasoned with that affectionate love required by the first rule, given above.

2. Carefully watch ourselves and others for the first signs of any beginnings of strife which are like the first escape of water that could result in the bursting of the dam.

3. Act carefully to smooth away the first appearance of any division, and if we fail in this, to consult the church.

4. Daily to strike at the root of all division, by striving for universal conformity to Jesus Christ.

Questions for consideration/discussion

1. Is your church *'of one heart and one soul'* (Acts 4:32)? If not, are you part of the reason? What could you do to improve matters?

2. In our days, evangelical churches are notorious for their 'splits'. Do we consider this to be a *certain dishonour of the Lord Jesus, a scandal to the gospel, a ruin of churches, and a shame and sorrow to the saints*, or rather a kind of 'occupational hazard' that must just be accepted?

3. What are the various causes of a church 'split'? How are they to be avoided?

4. Do you know of any case where a church was entrusted with the task of judging a civil or legal disagreement between some of its members? Does the rarity of such an event point to the inability of church officers to resolve such cases, or to the unwillingness of members to submit to a church ruling?

Rule 5

Believers are to separate and keep apart from the world, and from the men of the world in all their ways of false worship, so that we are seen to be a different people.

- Num. 23:9. Behold a people dwelling alone, and not counting itself among the nations.

- John 15:19. Because you are not of the world, but I chose you out of the world, therefore the world hates you.

- 2 Cor. 6:14-18. Do not be unequally yoked with unbelievers. For what partnership has righteousness with lawlessness? Or what fellowship has light with darkness? What accord has Christ with Belial? Or what portion does a believer share with an unbeliever? What agreement has the temple of God with idols? For we are the temple of the living God; as God said, 'I will make my dwelling among them and walk among them, and I will be their God, and they shall be my people. Therefore go out from their midst, and be separate from them, says the Lord, and I will be a father to you, and you shall be sons and daughters to me, says the Lord Almighty.'

- Eph. 5:8, 11. Walk as children of light… take no part in the unfruitful works of darkness.

- 2 Tim. 3:5. Having the appearance of godliness, but denying its power. Avoid such people.

- Hosea 4:15. Though you play the whore, O Israel, let not Judah become guilty. Enter not into Gilgal, nor go up to Beth-aven.

- Rev. 18:4. Come out of her, my people, lest you take part in her sins, lest you share in her plagues.

- Prov. 14:7. Leave the presence of a fool, for there you do not meet words of knowledge.

Explanation 5

The world does not sympathise much with those who separate from it, but there is a separation that is acceptable to the mind of God. Someone who will not separate from the world and from false worship has *separated himself* from Christ.

The separation that is commanded here is not referring in any way to the bonds of natural affections or for spiritual caring for the good of souls, Rom. 9:3; nor to the duties of social relationships, 1 Cor. 5:10; 1 Thess. 4:12; even less has it to do with seeking the good and prosperity of those in the world, 1 Tim. 2:1-2; communicating good things to them, Gal. 6:10; or living harmoniously and peaceably with them, Rom. 12:18. It relates, rather, to:

1. The way we walk and behave, Rom. 12:2; Eph. 4:17-20;

2. Any delight of conversation and familiarity in situations where enmity and opposition to the gospel exist, Eph. 5:3-4, 6-8, 10-11;

3. Ways of worship and acts of fellowship, Rev. 18:4; we are not to engage in any way with the excesses and idolatries of worldly religion.

These three commandments, and other similar indications of God's will, are very direct: the necessity of obeying them is evidently urgent. Our spiritual profit and prosperity make it equally necessary that we do so. Separation without a proper cause from churches that are established on true scriptural grounds (though perhaps failing in practice in matters of small concern) is no small sin; but separation from sinful practices and disorderly ways, and false unwarranted methods of worship, is a fulfilling of the command not to take part in other men's sins. To delight in the company, fellowship, society and conversation of dubious and headstrong people manifests a spirit that is not committed to Christ.

Motives for obeying this rule are:

1. God's command.

2. Our own preservation from sin and protection from punishment; that we should not be infected and share in the plague of others.

3. Christ's delight in the purity of his ordinances.

4. Christ's distinguishing love for his saints.

A necessary provision to be made is that, while obeying this rule, no unnecessary offence is to be given to anyone.

Questions for consideration/discussion

1. We are to be in the world but not of it (John 17:14-16). Here, again, a believer has to walk the narrow way between opposite extremes. Discuss examples of the different situations which would constitute failure to keep this rule due to insufficient

separation from the world on the one hand, or excessive separation on the other. The discussion might concentrate separately on (a) failure in our social interaction, and (b) failure in our worship.

2. This is an area where sincere believers may come to different conclusions as to what is lawful and what is not. 'Each one should be fully convinced in his own mind… For whatever does not proceed from faith is sin' (Rom. 14:5, 23). How can we ensure that our own standards are scriptural and not tending to worldliness?

3. The spectrum of church groupings and activities today provide the widest range imaginable of methods and practices of worship. Is the worship of your church governed by scriptural directions such as those quoted above, or are they not considered relevant in this context?

4. Both in the past and in the present, different Christian groupings have used the adjectives 'legalistic' and 'antinomian' as insults to hurl at one another. What do these two terms really mean? In your opinion, what practices truly are legalistic or antinomian in (a) our social interactions, (b) our worship?

Rule 6

Believers should engage in frequent spiritual conversation for edification, according to the measure of their gifts.

- Mal. 3:16. Then those who feared the LORD spoke with one another. The LORD paid attention and heard them, and a book of remembrance was written before him of those who feared the LORD and esteemed his name.

- Job 2:11. Now when Job's three friends heard of all this evil that had come upon him, they came each from his own place.... They made an appointment together to come to show him sympathy and comfort him.

- Eph. 4:29. Let no corrupting talk come out of your mouths, but only such as is good for building up, as fits the occasion, that it may give grace to those who hear.

- Col. 4:6. Let your speech always be gracious, seasoned with salt, so that you may know how you ought to answer each person.

- Eph. 5:4. Let there be no filthiness nor foolish talk nor crude joking, which are out of place, but instead let there be thanksgiving.

- 1 Thess. 5:11. Therefore encourage one another and build one another up, just as you are doing.

- Heb. 3:13. But exhort one another every day, as long as it is called 'today', that none of you may be hardened by the deceitfulness of sin.

- Jude 20. Build yourselves up in your most holy faith; pray in the Holy Spirit.

- Heb. 10:24-25. Let us consider how to stir up one another to love and good works, not neglecting to meet together, as is the habit of some, but encouraging one another, and all the more as you see the Day drawing near.

- Acts 18:26. When Priscilla and Aquila heard him, they took him and explained to him the way of God more accurately.

- 1 Cor. 12:7. To each is given the manifestation of the Spirit for the common good.

Explanation 6

That men who are not solemnly called and set apart to the office of public ministry might yet possess useful gifts for teaching was mentioned before. That a church should not make use of such gifts in an orderly way, according to the rule and custom of the church, would be to hide a talent given to be used and profited from. It is obvious that every person should make every effort to contribute and add to the culture and knowledge of his or her family. But it is just as obvious that we should labour to do so in the church also, the family of God.

The Scriptures given above show this; particularly with respect to the gifts of prayer, exhortation, instruction from the word and encouragement. The fulfilling of this duty of mutual edification is an obligation upon believers.

1. *Ordinarily*, Eph. 4:29, 5:3-4; Heb. 3:13. Believers, in their ordinary daily discourse, ought to be continually mentioning the Lord in helpful, profitable conversation, and not waste their opportunities with foolish, light, frothy words that are out of place.

2. *Occasionally*, Luke 24:14; Mal. 3:16. If providentially some circumstance of importance and relevance to the church should arise, a proper discussion of it amongst believers, for their own spiritual good, is necessary.

3. *By a special meeting* appointed for prayer and instruction from the word, Acts 10:24; 12:12; Job 2:11; Eph. 5:19; James 5:16; Jude 20; 1 Thess. 5:14. This would be an additional church meeting, specially called for the increasing of knowledge, love, experience, and the improving of the gifts of the church, with everyone contributing to the building of the tabernacle.

Let all useless talk be put away then. The time is short and the days are evil. Let us be convicted that we have neglected so many previous opportunities of growing in the knowledge of our Lord Jesus Christ and of doing good to one another. Let the rest of our few and evil days be spent in living for him who died for us. Be not conformed to this world, or to the people of this world.

Questions for consideration/discussion

1. Does John Owen mean that there is to be no 'small talk' between Christians?

2. What are the motives that keep us from the kind of spiritual conversation that he is describing?

3. How might these obstacles be overcome?

Rule 7

Believers must bear with one another's infirmities, weaknesses, sensitivities and failings, in meekness, patience and pity, and providing help and assistance.

- Eph. 4:32. Be kind to one another, tender-hearted, forgiving one another, as God in Christ forgave you.

- Matt. 18:21-22. Then Peter came up and said to him, 'Lord, how often will my brother sin against me, and I forgive him? As many as seven times?' Jesus said to him, 'I do not say to you seven times, but seventy times seven.'

- Mark 11:25-26. Whenever you stand praying, forgive, if you have anything against anyone, so that your Father also who is in heaven may forgive you your trespasses. But if you do not forgive, neither will your Father who is in heaven forgive your trespasses.

- Rom. 14:13. Therefore let us not pass judgement on one another any longer, but rather decide never to put a stumbling block or hindrance in the way of a brother.

- Rom. 15:1-2. We who are strong have an obligation to bear with the failings of the weak, and not to please ourselves. Let each of us please his neighbour for his good, to build him up.

- 1 Cor. 13:4-7. Love is patient and kind; love does not envy or boast; it is not arrogant or rude. It does not insist on its own way; it is not irritable or resentful; it does not rejoice at wrongdoing, but rejoices with the truth. Love bears all things, believes all things, hopes all things, endures all things.

- Gal. 6:1. Brothers, if anyone is caught in any transgression, you who are spiritual should restore him in a spirit of gentleness. Keep watch on yourself, lest you too be tempted.

- Col. 3:12-14. Put on then, as God's chosen ones, holy and beloved, compassionate hearts, kindness, humility, meekness, and patience, bearing with one another and, if one has a complaint against another, forgiving each other; as the Lord has forgiven you, so you also must forgive. And above all these put on love, which binds everything together in perfect harmony.

Explanation 7

'It is the glory of God to conceal things', Prov. 25:2. Free pardon is the substance of the gospel, the work of God in perfection, Isa. 55. It is presented to us for our imitation, Matt. 18:23-35. While we are still in the body we do everything imperfectly; freedom from failing is a fruit of glory. We now see dimly, as in a mirror; we know only in part. We all stumble in many ways; who knows how often? Bearing with mutual failings, pardoning offences, and supporting weaknesses—these few pence—may remind us of the talents forgiven us. Let him that is without fault throw stones at others.

Some men rejoice at the failings of others. They are malicious and fail more in their sinful joy than do their brothers of whom they are critical. Some are angry at weaknesses and infirmities. They are proud and conceited, not considering that they also are in the flesh. Some take delight in always dwelling continually on a frailty; they do not deserve to receive charity for their own weaknesses. Who is it who can bear an injury received seven times? Peter thought it too much. Some men think of revenge more than pardon. Some pretend to forgive, but yet every slight offence continues to alienate their affection and to keep them from fellowship. Some will hide a rough heart with a smooth face. Christ is not in any of these ways. They do not savour of the gospel. Meekness, patience, forbearance and forgiveness, hiding, covering, removing of offences—these are the footsteps of Christ.

Do you see your brother fail? Pity him. Does he continue in it? Earnestly pray for him; warn him. Cannot another man sin without you responding by sinning also? If you are angry, annoyed, rejoicing, estranged from him, you are a partner with him in the evil, instead of helping him. What if God were angry every time you gave him cause, and struck you every time you provoked him? When your brother offends you, hold your response until you have reminded yourself of the patience and forbearance of God towards you, and then consider his command to go and do likewise. Therefore, let all tenderness of affection and heart-felt compassion towards one another be put on amongst us, as becomes saints.

Let pity, not envy; mercy, not malice; patience, not passion; Christ, not flesh; grace, not nature; pardon, not spite or revenge, be our guides and companions in our fellowship.

Motives for obeying this rule are:

1. God's infinite mercy, patience, forbearance, long-suffering and free grace towards us; sparing, pardoning, pitying, bearing with us, in innumerable daily, hourly failings and provocations. Especially so when we consider that all this is set before us for our imitation to the best of our ability, Matt. 18:23-35.

2. The goodness, the unwearied and unchangeable love of the Lord Jesus Christ for us, continually pleading on our behalf, notwithstanding our continual backsliding, 1 John 2:1-2.

3. The experience which our own hearts have of the need in which we stand of the patience, forbearance and pardon of others, Eccles. 7:20-22.

4. The great glory of the gospel, which is displayed when brethren walk according to this rule.

Questions for consideration/discussion

1. John Owen gives good, practical advice on what to do when a fellow-believer offends us: *'hold your response until you have reminded yourself of the patience and forbearance of God towards you'*; consider *'the experience which our own hearts have of the need in which we stand of the patience, forbearance and pardon of others.'* What other steps have you found helpful when seeking to obey this rule?

2. A German word, *'Schadenfreude'*, is often used in English writings. Its literal meaning is 'harm-joy', a malicious joy in the misfortunes of others. It would seem to be a universal symptom of our fallen condition as human beings. How can a Christian overcome and eradicate this sin?

3. There are lists given above of the various virtues we need to 'put on' as Christians: *'compassion, kindness, humility, meekness, patience…'*; *'forbearance, forgiveness'*; *'a spirit of gentleness'*, for example. What are the practical steps to take that will help us as we seek to obey these commands?

Rule 8

Believers must support one another, tenderly and affectionately, in their various circumstances and conditions—bearing one another's burdens.

- Gal. 6:2. Bear one another's burdens, and so fulfil the law of Christ.

- Heb. 13:3. Remember those who are in prison, as though in prison with them, and those who are mistreated, since you also are in the body.

- 1 Cor. 12:25-26. That there may be no division in the body, but that the members may have the same care for one another. If one member suffers, all suffer together; if one member is honoured, all rejoice together.

- 2 Cor. 11:29. Who is weak, and I am not weak? Who is made to fall, and I am not indignant?

- James 1:27. Religion that is pure and undefiled before God, the Father, is this: to visit orphans and widows in their affliction, and to keep oneself unstained from the world.

- Matt. 25:35-36, 40. For I was hungry and you gave me food, I was thirsty and you gave me drink, I was a stranger and you welcomed me, I was naked and you clothed me, I was sick and you visited me, I was in prison and you came to me… Truly, I say to you, as you did it to one of the least of these my brothers, you did it to me.

- 2 Tim. 1:16-17. May the Lord grant mercy to the household of Onesiphorus, for he often refreshed me and was not ashamed of my chains, but when he arrived in Rome he searched for me earnestly and found me.

- Acts 20:35. In all things I have shown you that by working hard in this way we must help the weak and remember the words of the Lord Jesus, how he himself said, 'It is more blessed to give than to receive.'

Explanation 8

The previous rule concerned our attitude and response to our brothers in their failings; this rule deals with our response to their miseries and afflictions. Here again, conformity to Christ is required, who in all the afflictions of his people is afflicted, Isa. 63:9, and persecuted in their distresses, Acts 9:4.

If we could maintain a spiritual union to anything like the extent of the mutual union of the various parts of our physical bodies, which is the comparison so often made, this duty would be performed excellently. No one ever hated his own flesh. If one member is in pain, the others have very little comfort or ease. A member not affected by the anguish of its companions must be a rotten member. Those, enjoying plentiful comforts, who forget the miseries of their brethren are marked particularly for destruction,

Amos 6:4-7. If we do not feel the weight of our brothers' afflictions, burdens, and sorrows, then we deserve that our own should be doubled. The desolations of the church made Nehemiah grow pale in the court of the great king, Neh. 2:1-3. Those who are not concerned in the troubles, sorrows, trials, wants, poverties, and persecutions of the saints, not even so as to pity their wounds, to feel their blows, to refresh their spirits, to help bear their burdens upon their own shoulders, can never assure themselves that they are united to the head of those saints.

What is required in order to discharge this duty faithfully is:

1. A proper evaluation of, and a high respect for, the church's prosperity in every member of the church, and a strong desire for it, Psa. 122:6.

2. A heart of compassion as a fruit of love; to be aware of and deeply moved by the various burdens of the saints, Col. 3:12.

3. Courage and boldness to acknowledge the saints in all situations without shame, 2 Tim. 1:16-17.

4. Personal visits in sickness, troubles and difficulties, to advise, comfort and refresh them, Matt. 25:36.

5. Suitable support by administering temporal and spiritual assistance for their situation.

The motives for obeying this rule are the same as those for the preceding rule.

Questions for consideration/discussion

1. Are the means in place in your church for members to be aware of one another's burdens?

2. List the various burdens that might weigh upon believers—loneliness, illness, shame, etc. In what way could these be supported by other members of the church?

3. The verses quoted deal not only with our support for fellow-believers but also of strangers (Matt. 25:35-36). How welcoming is your church, or how welcoming are you, to strangers? How long would a stranger have to attend your church before he or she felt accepted as one of the congregation?—a week? a month? a year? or longer?

Rule 9

Believers are voluntarily to contribute and share in temporal things with those who are truly poor, in a way that is suitable to their necessities, wants and afflictions.

▪ 1 John 3:17-18. But if anyone has the world's goods and sees his brother in need, yet closes his heart against him, how does God's love abide in him? Little children, let us not love in word or talk but in deed and in truth.

- 1 Cor. 16:1-2. Now concerning the collection for the saints: as I directed to the churches of Galatia, so you also are to do. On the first day of every week, each of you is to put something aside and store it up, as he may prosper.

- 2 Cor. 9:5-7. So I thought it necessary to urge the brothers to go on ahead to you and arrange in advance for the gift you have promised, so that it may be ready as a willing gift, not as an exaction. The point is this: whoever sows sparingly will also reap sparingly, and whoever sows bountifully will also reap bountifully. Each one must give as he has decided in his heart, not reluctantly or under compulsion, for God loves a cheerful giver. (See the whole of chapters 8 and 9 of this epistle.)

- Rom. 12:13. Contribute to the needs of the saints and seek to show hospitality.

- Gal. 6:10. So then, as we have opportunity, let us do good to everyone, and especially to those who are of the household of faith.

- 1 Tim. 6:17-19. As for the rich in this present age, charge them not to be haughty, nor to set their hopes on the uncertainty of riches, but on God, who richly provides us with everything to enjoy. They are to do good, to be rich in good works, to be generous and ready to share, thus storing up treasure for themselves as a good foundation for the future, so that they may take hold of that which is truly life.

- Heb. 13:16. Do not neglect to do good and to share what you have, for such sacrifices are pleasing to God.

- Lev. 25:35. If your brother becomes poor and cannot maintain himself with you, you shall support him as though he were a stranger and a sojourner, and he shall live with you.

- Matt. 25:34-36, 40. Come, you who are blessed by my Father, inherit the kingdom prepared for you from the foundation of the world. For I was hungry and you gave me food, I was thirsty and you gave me drink, I was a stranger and you welcomed me, I was naked and you clothed me, I was sick and you visited me, I was in prison and you came to me…. Truly, I say to you, as you did it to one of the least of these my brothers, you did it to me.

Explanation 9

The fact that we will always have the poor with us according to the Saviour's prediction, Matt. 26:11, and to God's promise, Deut. 15:11, serves as a trial both of themselves and of ourselves: a trial of their contentedness in Christ alone and their submission to the all-disposing sovereignty of God; a trial of how freely we can part, for Christ's sake, with those things which have been given us. When God gave manna for food to his people, everyone had an equal share, Exod.

16:18, 'Whoever gathered much had nothing left over, and whoever gathered little had no lack'; 2 Cor. 8:15. This equality of distribution was practised again in the apostles' days, because of the need of the church, Acts 4:35. Out of the sum total of the believers' possessions a distribution was made to everyone according to his need.

It is perfectly true that, by God's appointment and providence, everyone has an individual right to the use and disposal of the earthly things trusted to him. The very precepts themselves that encourage free distribution and liberality are enough to prove this. But that these things are given in their entirety to men for themselves and their own use is denied; friends are to be made of mammon. Christ requires from some that which he will bestow on others. If he has given to you both your own and your brother's portion to keep, will you be false to your trust, and defraud your brother? Christ, being rich, became poor for our sakes; if he now makes us rich, it is in order that we may feed the poor for his sake. And this duty does not only lie with those who are rich (although it does predominantly); those who have nothing but the wages for the work of their hands should, out of that, spare something for those who cannot work, Eph. 4:28. The two mites are required as well as accepted.

The rule for the relief of the poor in the church is twofold: firstly, it is with respect to their own necessity; secondly, it is with respect to the ability of others. All assistance given must be in proportion to these two circumstances, provided that those who are poor are truly so, 2 Thess. 3:10-11. Just as we are to relieve men in their poverty, so we ought by all lawful means help them from becoming poor. To keep a man from falling is as much a mercy as helping him when he is down.

Motives for obeying this rule are:

1. The love of God to us, 1 John 3:16.

2. The glory of the gospel is greatly honoured by it, Titus 3:8, 14; Matt. 5:7.

3. The union into which we are brought in Christ, with all the common inheritance promised to every believer.

4. The testimony of the Lord Jesus that what is done in this way is done to himself, Matt. 25:35-40.

5. The promise attached to it, Eccles. 11:1; Prov. 19:17; Deut. 15:10; Matt. 10:42.

The means for fulfilling this rule is by appointing men, Acts 6:1-6, who will take what is voluntarily contributed by believers on the first day of the week, as God has prospered them, 1 Cor. 16:2, and to distribute to the needs of the saints, according to the guidance of the church. In addition, we all ought to abound in private charitable giving, Matt. 6:3; Heb. 13:16.

Questions for consideration/discussion

1. Do you agree that a church today requires the functioning of a group of men as described by John Owen in his last paragraph above? Has your church

---

such a group—a 'diaconate', 'eldership', 'pastor's fund committee' or whatever other name might be used—that performs this task?

2. *'For you always have the poor with you'* (Matt. 26:11). What obligations arise from this statement for, (a) a church, and (b) an individual believer? How are these obligations affected when the state provides welfare benefits and grants?

3. The rule contains the phrases, *'truly poor'*, and *'in a way that is suitable to their necessities, wants and afflictions'*. What do these words mean in practice?

4. If there are no *'truly poor'* within a particular congregation, or within one's own immediate circle of family, friends and acquaintances, what should a church or individual believer do?

Rule 10

Believers ought to note watchfully and avoid carefully all causes and causers of divisions; they are particularly to shun seducers, false teachers and those who spread heresies and errors that are contrary to the word of God.

- Rom. 16:17-18. I appeal to you, brothers, to watch out for those who cause divisions and create obstacles contrary to the doctrine that you have been taught; avoid them. For such persons do not serve our Lord Christ, but their own appetites, and by smooth talk and flattery they deceive the hearts of the naive.

- Matt. 24:4-5, 23-25. And Jesus answered them, 'See that no one leads you astray. For many will come in my name, saying, 'I am the Christ', and they will lead many astray... Then if anyone says to you, 'Look, here is the Christ!' or 'There he is!' do not believe it. For false christs and false prophets will arise and perform great signs and wonders, so as to lead astray, if possible, even the elect.'

- 1 Tim. 6:3-5. If anyone teaches a different doctrine and does not agree with the sound words of our Lord Jesus Christ and the teaching that accords with godliness, he is puffed up with conceit and understands nothing. He has an unhealthy craving for controversy and for quarrels about words, which produce envy, dissension, slander, evil suspicions, and constant friction among people who are depraved in mind and deprived of the truth, imagining that godliness is a means of gain.

- 2 Tim. 2:16-17. But avoid irreverent babble, for it will lead people into more and more ungodliness, and their talk will spread like gangrene.

- Tit. 3:9-11. But avoid foolish controversies... and quarrels about the law, for they are unprofitable and worthless. As for a person who stirs up division, after warning him once and then twice, have nothing more to do with him, knowing that such a person is warped and sinful; he is self-condemned.

- 1 John 2:18-19. Children, it is the last hour, and as you have heard that antichrist is coming, so now many antichrists have come. Therefore we know that it is the last hour. They went out from us, but they were not of us; for if they had been of us, they would have continued with us. But they went out, that it might become plain that they all are not of us.

- 1 John 4:1. Beloved, do not believe every spirit, but test the spirits to see whether they are from God, for many false prophets have gone out into the world.

- 2 John 10–11. If anyone comes to you and does not bring this teaching, do not receive him into your house or give him any greeting, for whoever greets him takes part in his wicked works.

- Acts 20:29-31. I know that after my departure fierce wolves will come in among you, not sparing the flock; and from among your own selves will arise men speaking twisted things, to draw away the disciples after them. Therefore, be alert...

- Rev. 2:14-16. But I have a few things against you: you have some there who hold the teaching of Balaam... So also you have some who hold the teaching of the

Nicolaitans. Therefore repent. If not, I will come to you soon and war against them with the sword of my mouth.

Explanation 10

The first phrase of this rule was discussed in part under Section 2, Rule 4. If the preservation of unity ought to be our aim, then certainly the causes and agents of division ought to be avoided. 'Avoid such people.' There is a generation of men whose tongues seem to be operated by the devil; James calls it, 'Set on fire by hell', James 3:6. As if they were the offspring of serpents, their greatest delight is in the fire of controversy; they live on disputing, quarrelling, backbiting and endless strivings. 'Note such men and avoid them.' Usually they are men with private interests, worldly goals, high conceits and proud spirits. 'From such turn away.'

For the latter part of the rule, respecting seducers, it is clear that a judgement of discerning by the Spirit rests in the church and in its individual members, 1 John 2:27; 1 Cor. 2:15; Isa. 8:20. They are commanded to exercise this duty, 1 John 4:1; 1 Cor. 14:29; it is commended to them, Acts 17:11; and they are encouraged in it, Phil. 1:9-10; Heb. 5:14.

'If the blind lead the blind, both will fall into a pit.' That gold which refuses to be tested may well be suspected. Christians must choose the good and refuse the evil. If false teachers succeed in leading them astray it will not be long before those teachers will require blind submission from them.

For believers to perform this duty and obey this rule correctly, it is necessary:

1. That their minds should be exercised in the word, 'trained by constant practice to distinguish good from evil', Heb. 5:14; especially, that they obtain from the Scriptures a 'pattern of the sound words', 2 Tim. 1:13, of the main truths of the gospel and the fundamental doctrines of religion. They will then, at the first appearance of anything unorthodox, be able to turn away from its advocate and 'not give him any greeting'.

2. That they listen and pay attention only to what comes to them in God's way. Some men, or even very many in our days, have such a delight in novelties that they run greedily after everyone who would deceive them with plausible arguments, propagating some new pretended revelations. They excuse themselves by saying that they have a freedom, even a duty, of trying all things, not appreciating that God would have his own work done only in his own way. They do not stop to inquire after the qualifications of these false teachers. Most of the seducers and false prophets of our days seem to be men who are not in God's way, leaving their own vocations to wander without a call—ordinary or extraordinary—without providence or promise. If believers voluntarily, without reason, give themselves to listen and attend to them, they are tempting God, who justly and with every right may then deliver them up to the effects of error, allowing them to believe the

lies that they hear. Listen, and test, only that which comes to you in God's way. Do not give any welcome to anything else.

3. That they know, and always keep in mind, the nature of these seducers who would win over unstable souls. The Holy Spirit has described to us that nature in the word: firstly, that they will come in 'sheep's clothing', Matt. 7:15, with fine pretences of innocence and holiness; secondly, with 'smooth talk and flattery', Rom. 16:17-18, smooth as butter and oil; thirdly, bringing doctrines that are suited to some treasured lust of men, especially the hope of a broad and easy way of salvation; fourthly, with pretences of glorious discoveries and revelations, Matt. 24:24; 2 Thess. 2:2.

4. That they utterly reject and separate from those who have been warned and disciplined by the church, Titus 3:10.

5. That they do not receive any teacher or preacher who has not been approved by men of known integrity in the church. In these evil days men will run to hear new teachers even though they do not know where they come from or what they are. The laudable practice of the first churches was to give testimonials to those who were to travel from one place to another, 1 Cor. 16:3, and not to receive anyone without them, Acts 9:26. Today, this practice seems to be quite forgotten.

6. That they live in observance of the law, not paying attention to the doctrine of anyone who is not known and approved by the churches.

7. That they put away any delight in novelties, controversies, dissensions, and all teaching that does not accord with godliness; these can very often prove to be the starting-points of awful apostasies, Titus 3:9; 2 Tim. 4:3; 1 Tim. 6:3-5.

Questions for consideration/discussion

1. The phrase *'in God's way'* crops up often in note 2 of the explanation. What does John Owen mean by it?

2. How may we discern between those who teach error inadvertently because of inadequate knowledge (Acts 18:24-28), and those teaching error because they are *'not of us'* (1 John 2:19)?

3. A young believer hears a speaker or friend arguing for a doctrine that is quite new to him. What should he do?

4. What is the procedure in your church for receiving into membership someone who has previously been a member in another Christian church?

Rule 11

Believers should cheerfully accept the lot and portion of the whole church, in prosperity and affliction, and not draw back for any reason whatever.

- Matt. 13:20-21. As for what was sown on rocky ground, this is the one who hears the word and immediately receives it with joy, yet he has no root in himself, but endures for a while, and when tribulation or persecution arises on account of the word, immediately he falls away.

- Heb. 10:23-25, 32-39. Let us hold fast the confession of our hope without wavering, for he who promised is faithful. And let us consider how to stir up one another to love and good works, not neglecting to meet together, as is the habit of some, but encouraging one another, and all the more as you see the Day drawing near.... But recall the former days when, after you were enlightened, you endured a hard struggle with sufferings, sometimes being publicly exposed to reproach and affliction, and sometimes being partners with those so treated. For you had compassion on those in prison, and you joyfully accepted the plundering of your property, since you knew that you yourselves had a better possession and an abiding one. Therefore do not throw away your confidence, which has a great reward. For you have need of endurance, so that when you have done the will of God you may receive what is promised. For, 'Yet a little while, and the coming one will come and will not delay; but my righteous one shall live by faith, and if he shrinks back, my soul has no pleasure in him.' But we are not of those who shrink back and are destroyed, but of those who have faith and preserve their souls.

- 2 Tim. 4:10, 16. For Demas, in love with this present world, has deserted me… At my first defence no one came to stand by me, but all deserted me. May it not be charged against them.

Explanation 11

To backslide from the practice of any of the teachings of Christ, or the use of his ordinances, having been convinced that these were instituted by him, is a considerable apostasy from Christ himself.

Apostasy, in whatever degree, results in the offence to God of a refusing of the sweetness and goodness found in Christ and a turning instead to transitory things. Backsliders nearly always have their excuses. Usually, like Lot of Zoar, they excuse their lapses by comparing them to what they still pretend to maintain, saying, 'It is a little one.' But, without exception, we find that such things lead universally to more ungodliness. Every unrecovered step backwards from the ways of Jesus Christ reveals the unfaithfulness of the heart, whatever former professions there may have been.

Those who, from whatever motives, are tempted to look for excuses for neglecting gospel duties in order to gain temporal benefits, will always find some ready at hand.

The beginnings of great evils are to be resisted. We have already mentioned that this neglect of gospel duties (which always involves a contempt of the communion of the saints) has been the main cause of the great dishonour and confusion into which most churches in the world have fallen. This is because it is a righteous thing with God to allow professing believers to become futile in their thinking, if neither the love of Christ nor the terror of the Lord can keep them from the fear of men.

May this, therefore, together with the danger and abomination of backsliding, make such an impression on the hearts of saints, that 'with steadfast purpose' they will 'remain steadfast to the Lord' and 'follow hard after him' in all the ordinances. If, then, persecutions arise, they may cheerfully 'follow the Lamb wherever he goes', and by sticking closely to one another may receive such mutual assistance and support that their joint prayers may prevail with the goodness of God, and their joint suffering overcome the wickedness of men.

Motives for obeying this rule of a close adherence to the church in which we are in fellowship in all circumstances, are:

1. The pre-eminence and excellence of the ordinances we enjoy.

2. The danger of backsliding and the evidence of unfaithfulness that the smallest degree of it provides.

3. The scandal, confusion and disorder of the church that results if this rule is neglected.

Questions for consideration/discussion

1. Notice that John Owen points to *'the love of Christ'* and *'the terror of the Lord'* as the two motivating factors that keep believers from backsliding. In today's climate of multiple apostasies, which of these two factors has decreased most in its influence over the churches?

2. Our Christian confidence (Heb. 10:35) has *'a great reward'*. In times of unbelief, affliction and persecution, what steps should be taken by a church to increase this confidence in its members, ensuring their endurance and faithful perseverance?

3. A professing believer has begun to absent himself from the church services. How may a church, or the believer himself for that matter, discern whether this is a temporary period of backsliding, or the beginning of a complete apostasy?

Rule 12

In church affairs, believers must not discriminate between persons but condescend to the weakest brother and perform the least service, for the good of fellow-believers.

- James 2:1-6. My brothers, show no partiality as you hold the faith in our Lord Jesus Christ, the Lord of glory. For if a man wearing a gold ring and fine clothing comes into your assembly, and a poor man in shabby clothing also comes in, and if you pay attention to the one who wears the fine clothing and say, 'You sit here in a good place', while you say to the poor man, 'You stand over there', or, 'Sit down at my feet', have you not then made distinctions among yourselves and become judges with evil thoughts? Listen, my beloved brothers, has not God chosen those who are poor in the world to be rich in faith and heirs of the kingdom, which he has promised to those who love him? But you have dishonoured the poor man.

- Matt. 20:26-27. It shall not be so among you. But whoever would be great among you must be your servant, and whoever would be first among you must be your slave.

- Rom. 12:16. Live in harmony with one another. Do not be haughty, but associate with the lowly. Never be wise in your own sight.

- John 13:12-16. When he had washed their feet and put on his outer garments and resumed his place, he said to them, 'Do you understand what I have done to you? You call me Teacher and Lord, and you are right, for so I am. If I then, your Lord and Teacher, have washed your feet, you also ought to wash one another's feet. For I have given you an example, that you also should do just as I have done to you. Truly, truly, I say to you, a servant is not greater than his master, nor is a messenger greater than the one who sent him.'

Explanation 12

Where the Lord has not discriminated, neither should we. In Jesus Christ there is neither rich nor poor, high nor low, but a new creature. Generally speaking, 'God chose what is weak in the world to shame the strong.'

Experience teaches us that not many wise according to worldly standards, not many powerful, not many of noble birth are partakers of the heavenly calling. It is not that Christ's gospel contradicts or removes these differences and distinctions between men—distinctions arising from power, authority, relationships, enjoyments of earthly blessings, gifts, age, or any other factor, according to the institution and appointment of God; nor does the gospel do away with the respect, reverence, duty, obedience and subjection due to such people of distinction; even less does it destroy the established bounds of propriety and ownership of earthly things. But it declares that, in matters which are spiritual, these outward things, which on the whole are the same for all, are of no value or esteem. All believers are to be considered as saints, and not as great or rich. All are equal, all are naked, before God.

Free grace is the only thing that distinguishes; all are brothers in the same family, servants of the same master, employed in the same work, acted upon by the same precious faith, enjoying the same purchased privileges, expecting the same recompense of reward and eternal life. Why should any differences arise? Therefore, let the greatest consider it their greatest honour to perform the lowest necessary service on behalf of the lowest of the saints. A spiritual community should ensure equality in spiritual matters. It is not the richest person, nor the poorest person, but the humblest person, who is accepted before the Lord.

Motives for obeying this rule are:

1. Christ's example.

2. The commandments of Scripture.

3. The fact that God does not discriminate between persons.

4. Our joint possession of the same, common faith, hope, etc.

5. The irrelevance of all causes of outward differences when it comes to the things of God.

Questions for consideration/discussion

1. In what ways in a church congregation might the discrimination described above be present?

2. *'For I have given you an example, that you also should do just as I have done to you.'* Discuss the various ways, in the context of church life, in which we might follow the Saviour's example. In how many of these do we personally participate?

3. 'Toadies, sycophants, crawlers, back-scratchers, flunkeys, hangers-on...'—the English language is rich in words describing those guilty of one type of discrimination. Discuss the wrong motivations which tempt us into such behaviour.

Rule 13

If any member is in distress, persecution, or affliction, the whole church is to be humbled, and to be earnest in prayer on his behalf.

- Acts 12:5, 7, 12. So Peter was kept in prison, but earnest prayer for him was made to God by the church... And behold, an angel of the Lord stood next to him, and a light shone in the cell. He struck Peter on the side and woke him up, saying, 'Get up quickly.' And the chains fell off his hands... When he realized this, he went to the house of Mary, the mother of John whose other name was Mark, where many were gathered together and were praying.

- Rom. 12:15. Rejoice with those who rejoice, weep with those who weep.

- 1 Cor. 12:26-27. If one member suffers, all suffer together; if one member is honoured, all rejoice together. Now you are the body of Christ and individually members of it.

- 2 Thess. 3:1-2. Finally, brothers, pray for us… that we may be delivered from wicked and evil men.

Explanation 13

This duty is, on the whole, included in previous rules and we do not therefore need to discuss it fully; especially as, on the understanding of being fellow-members, it is no more than would naturally be required. God is as delighted by his churches' fervent prayers as by their thankful praises. He therefore calls them, by his various providences, to fulfil this duty. In order to spare the whole church, he will sometimes afflict one or another of its members, knowing that the close relationship between the members, established by him and wrought by his Spirit, will produce a common distress and combined prayer.

Spiritual union is nobler and more excellent than natural union, but this means that it would be reprehensible if any one member, or the whole church in general, did not suffer with, and care for, the distress of every part and member. Any one member who does not feel the pains of its fellows is rotten, and should be cut off, in case it infects the remainder of the body.

Therefore if any members of the church are under the weight of God's afflicting hand, or the persecuting rage of man, it is the duty of every fellow-member, and of the church as a whole, to be aware of it, and to consider themselves as sharers in it, so as to be continually in earnest prayer to God, and be at hand to provide every suitable assistance. In this way they are to show their spiritual concern in the affliction.

This should be so in order that:

Firstly, the will of God is fulfilled. Secondly, the glory of the gospel is exalted. Thirdly, the preservation and deliverance of the whole church is obtained. Fourthly, the saints secure a degree of conformity with the sufferings of Christ. Fifthly, the inestimable benefits of church-fellowship are enjoyed.

Questions for consideration/discussion

1. Does your church—by its individual members in private and by its combined prayers in public—offer up earnest prayers for fellow-members suffering affliction?

2. Do you suffer when any member of your congregation suffers, or only when those closest to you suffer?

Rule 14

Believers must watch one another's behaviour carefully and warn one another to avoid all disorderly conduct. If any offending member will not accept such warning their case must be brought to the church.

- Matt. 18:15-17. If your brother sins against you, go and tell him his fault, between you and him alone. If he listens to you, you have gained your brother. But if he does not listen, take one or two others along with you, that every charge may be established by the evidence of two or three witnesses. If he refuses to listen to them, tell it to the church.

- 1 Thess. 5:14. And we urge you, brothers, admonish the idle, encourage the faint-hearted, help the weak, be patient with them all.

- Heb. 3:12-13. Take care, brothers, lest there be in any of you an evil, unbelieving heart, leading you to fall away from the living God. But exhort one another every day, as long as it is called 'today', that none of you may be hardened by the deceitfulness of sin.

- Heb. 10:24-25. And let us consider how to stir up one another to love and good works… encouraging one another, and all the more as you see the Day drawing near.

- Heb. 12:13, 15-16. Make straight paths for your feet, so that what is lame may not be put out of joint but rather be healed… See to it that no one fails to obtain the grace of God; that no 'root of bitterness' springs up and causes trouble, and by it many become defiled; that no one is sexually immoral or unholy like Esau, who sold his birthright for a single meal.

- Lev. 19:17. You shall not hate your brother in your heart, but you shall reason frankly with your neighbour, lest you incur sin because of him.

- 2 Thess. 3:15. Do not regard him as an enemy, but warn him as a brother.

- Rom. 15:14. I myself am satisfied about you, my brothers, that you yourselves are full of goodness, filled with all knowledge and able to instruct one another.

- James 5:19-20. My brothers, if anyone among you wanders from the truth and someone brings him back, let him know that whoever brings back a sinner from his wandering will save his soul from death and will cover a multitude of sins.

- Prov. 29:1. He who is often reproved, yet stiffens his neck, will suddenly be broken beyond healing.

Explanation 14

There is a threefold duty involved in this rule; the main

one, the one to be emphasized, is that of warning. The first duty, that of watching, precedes warning; and the third, that of referring to the church, follows only if a warning is ignored. Whether out of consideration of the glory of God and the gospel, or of the bonds of fellowship, the mutual love that exists between believers and the mutual obligation upon them to seek each other's good and spiritual profit, this duty is a great necessity and of great usefulness. Not that we should pry with curiosity into one another's failings, much less search maliciously for discoveries which would trouble and dishonour our brothers. Both of these actions are contrary to that love which 'thinks no evil' but rather will 'cover a multitude of sins'. We should observe one another's walk out of a sense of the glory of God, of the honour of the gospel, and out of concern for each other's souls. What is exemplary in another's behaviour should be followed, what is failing should be pointed out, and what is wrong may be reproved, that in all things God may be glorified and Christ exalted.

There are two methods of warning:

1. Warning authoritatively—by way of power;

2. Warning fraternally—by way of love.

The first of these again has two parts: firstly, doctrinally, by teaching; and secondly, by disciplining. Both of these actions involve the whole church and are not relevant here. The second also is twofold: a fraternal warning may be given as an exhortation, i.e. as an encouragement to do good; or it may be given as an admonition, i.e. as a reproof for something which is wrong. It is this last example which is particularly intended in this rule. Here, therefore, is the duty of every church member towards those with whom he walks in fellowship: that by using God's Word, he should admonish any member who he judges is, in some particular, not living according to the right way, and he is to do so with the one purpose of recovering that member's soul.

It is granted that much caution and wisdom, tenderness and moderation, is required by anyone performing this duty. A lack of these virtues means that matters can easily degenerate from a peaceful remedy of evil into the fuel of strife and debate. Anyone who is called to this duty should therefore consider the following points:

1. That at all times he should not transgress that rule of love which is given us, 1 Cor. 13:7; Gal. 6:2.

2. That he should maintain peace in his own heart by being assured that he is constantly labouring to cast out all the logs and specks in his own eye, Matt. 7:5.

3. That he should carry out the admonishing in such a way that it is always clear that he has no other purpose but the glory of God and the good of his brother, that all envy and rejoicing in evil is very far from him.

4. That he should make sure that he draws his warnings from the word, so that the authority of God accompanies them, and let him not presume to make any comment without the word.

5. That all the circumstances of the situation, of time, place, persons, etc., be weighed up and considered, so that the slightest provocation may be avoided.

6. That it is a practice in which Christ has a special regard.

7. That he should carefully distinguish between personal injuries to himself (which must be discussed in a context of forgiveness rather than reproof) and other offences that are more public.

8. Lastly, that self-examination with respect to the same or similar failings must always accompany any brotherly warning.

With these and similar points having been considered, let every believer, with Christian courage, admonish from the word, everyone whom they judge is failing in his Christian walk in any way, not willing that they should continue in sin. They are to be ready to hear, receive and be satisfied by a just defence or a promised amendment in behaviour. If such admonishing is not carried out in a case where a true offence is involved, a believer cannot be free from the guilt of other men's sins.

The believer who is being admonished should accept the warning, with all Christian patience, with no more anger or bitterness than he would feel should someone have broken a weapon by which he was about to be killed; and he should consider:

1. The authority of the one who has appointed this practice.

2. The privilege and mercy that he enjoys by such a spiritual prevention of a danger or evil which he himself perhaps was not aware of.

3. The dreadful judgements which are so often threatened towards those who despise reproofs, Prov. 29:1; so as to be able to accept thankfully a just admonition from the least member of the church congregation.

On the last point of the rule—resorting to the church when private admonition does not prevail—our Saviour has so plainly described in Matthew 18:15-17 the way to proceed that it needs no further explanation. I will only note that the word 'church' in verse 17 cannot be understood to mean the elders of the church alone but rather the whole congregation. Otherwise, if the offended brother takes with him two or three elders to interview the offender, as he is encouraged to do, then he has taken the 'church' with him, and the 'church' has been told of the offence before the reproof has been delivered by two or three. This would obviously be contrary to the rule.

Questions for consideration/discussion

1. Of all the rules in this manual, this is probably the one that is least implemented in our day and age. Why do you think this is?

2. What are the wrong ways to go about this reproving? And what would be the dangers that might result?

---

3. What are the right ways to do it? And what are the benefits that would follow?

4. Do you feel any personal responsibility in the spiritual failure of any church member?

5. John Owen gives far more attention to this rule than to any of the other twenty-one that he lists. Why do you think this might be?

Rule 15

Believers should live and walk in an exemplary way in all holiness and godliness, to the glory of the gospel, the edification of the church, and the conviction of those outside the church.

- Psa. 24:3-4. Who shall ascend the hill of the Lord? And who shall stand in his holy place? He who has clean hands and a pure heart, who does not lift up his soul to what is false and does not swear deceitfully.

- Matt. 5:16, 20. Let your light shine before others, so that they may see your good works and give glory to your Father who is in heaven… For I tell you, unless your righteousness exceeds that of the scribes and the Pharisees, you will never enter the kingdom of heaven.

- Matt. 21:19. And seeing a fig tree by the wayside, he

went to it and found nothing on it but only leaves. And he said to it, 'May no fruit ever come from you again!' And the fig tree withered at once.

- 2 Tim. 2:19. Let everyone who names the name of the Lord depart from iniquity.

- Titus 2:11-14. For the grace of God has appeared, bringing salvation for all people, training us to renounce ungodliness and worldly passions, and to live self-controlled, upright, and godly lives in the present age, waiting for our blessed hope, the appearing of the glory of our great God and Saviour Jesus Christ, who gave himself for us to redeem us from all lawlessness and to purify for himself a people for his own possession who are zealous for good works.

- Eph. 4:21-23. Assuming that you have heard about him and were taught in him, as the truth is in Jesus, to put off your old self, which belongs to your former manner of life and is corrupt through deceitful desires, and to be renewed in the spirit of your minds.

- 1 Pet. 3:1-2. Likewise, wives, be subject to your own husbands, so that even if some do not obey the word, they may be won without a word by the conduct of their wives, when they see your respectful and pure conduct.

- Heb. 12:14. Strive for peace with everyone, and for the holiness without which no one will see the Lord.

- Eph. 5:15-16. Look carefully then how you walk, not as unwise but as wise, making the best use of the time, because the days are evil.

- 2 Sam. 12:14. Nevertheless, because by this deed you have utterly scorned the LORD, the child who is born to you shall die.

Explanation 15

Holiness befits the house of the Lord forever, without it no one will see the Lord. Christ died to wash his church, to present it before his Father without spot or blemish; to purchase to himself a people for his own possession who are zealous for good works. It is by the kingdom of God which is within us that we appear to all to be the children of God. This, then, should be the great differentiating character of the church in the world, that they are a holy, humble, self-denying people. Our master is holy; his doctrine and worship are holy; let us make every effort to ensure that our hearts also are holy.

This is the wisdom that we show to those who are outside the church, by which they may be guided or convicted; this is the means by which we build one another up effectively. Examples are a more convincing way of instruction than precepts. Loose living, which causes the name of God to be blasphemed, the little ones of Christ to be offended, and his enemies to rejoice, results in the most miserable of sorrows. O that all who are called to a holy life and who enjoy holy ordinances, might also shine in holy behaviour, so that those who accuse them of being evil-doers might have their mouths stopped and their hearts filled with shame, to the glory of the gospel!

This general rule involves walking wisely, in all patience, meekness and long-suffering towards unbelievers, until they show themselves to be those who fight against God, at which point they are to be prayed for. The rule also includes the necessary patience of the saints in all their tribulations, sufferings and persecutions for the name of Christ.

Motives for obeying this rule and for continuing to exercise holiness, in our internal and external actions, private and public life, personal and public relationships, are:

1. The utter insufficiency of the most precious ordinances to provide any communion with God without it.

2. The miserable fate of those who have been deceived by a barren, empty, fruitless faith.

3. The glory of the gospel, when its power has an evident effect on the hearts, thoughts, words, actions and lives of believers.

4. The scandal of the gospel, the advantage to its enemies, the shame of the church, and the fierce wrath of God, which result from the unholy lives of believers.

5. The sweet reward which the practice of holiness brings along with it, even in this life, together with that eternal weight of glory to which it leads in the future. To

which, may the holy Son of God bring us all, through the sprinkling of his most holy blood!

Questions for consideration/discussion

1. How is holiness to be sought after? Is growth in holiness something that is given by God or is it worked out by the believer?

2. In the light of Matt. 5:16, are we to emphasize our good deeds, pointing them out to our friends and acquaintances?

3. What is the message of the occasion when Christ cursed the fig tree? (Matt. 21:18-19; Mark 11:12-14, 20-21).

4. John Owen clearly considered that the last five motives that he gives above provide an appropriate conclusion and end to his manual on church fellowship. Why do you think he might have thought so?

The Banner of Truth Trust originated in 1957 in London. The founders believed that much of the best literature of historic Christianity had been allowed to fall into oblivion and that, under God, its recovery could well lead not only to a strengthening of the church, but to true revival.

Inter-denominational in vision, this publishing work is now international, and our lists include a number of contemporary authors along with classics from the past. The translation of these books into many languages is encouraged.

A monthly magazine, *The Banner of Truth*, is also published. More information about this and all our publications can be found on our website or supplied by either of the offices below.

THE BANNER OF TRUTH TRUST

3 Murrayfield Road
Edinburgh, EH12 6EL
UK

PO Box 621, Carlisle
Pennsylvania 17013
USA

www.banneroftruth.org